I0427440

RON DESANTIS

Ron Desantis's Leadership Style: Strategies And

Decision-making Approachess

Don T. Hart

Ron desantis

All right reserved. No part of this publication may be reproduced, distributed or transmitted in any form or by any means, including photocopyng,recording or other electronic or mechanical methods without the prio written permission of the publisher, except in the case of brief quotation embodied in critical revews and certain other noncommercial uses permitted by copy right laws

Copyright © Don T Hart 2024

Ron desantis

Table of contents

INTRODUCTION

      CHAPTER 1. Who is Ron Desantis?

1.1 OVERVIEW OF RON DESANTIS'S POLITICAL JOURNEY

      CHAPTER 2. LEADERSHIP FOUNDATION.

2.1 MILITARY INFLUENCE: THE SHAPING OF A LEADER

2.2 CONGREGATIONAL YEARS OF RON DESANTIS: EARLY INDICATORS OF LEADERSHIP STYLES.

      CHAPTER 3. CORE PRINCIPLES AND VALUES.

3.1 COMMITMENT TO INDIVIDUAL FREEDOMS.

3.2 ECONOMIC PHILOSOPHY:GROWTH AND PROSPERITY..

Ron desantis

3.3 ENVIRONMENTAL STEWARDSHIP

CHAPTER 4. DECISION MAKING

 FRAMEWORK

4.1 PRAGMATISM IN POLICY CHOICES.

4.2 CRISIS MANAGEMENT: DESANTIS

RESPONSE TO CHALLENGES.

4.3 TRANSPARENCY

4.4 ACCOUNTABILITY

CHAPTER 5. COMMUNICATION

STRATEGIES

5.1 STAND UP FOR YOUR BELIEFS

5.2: BE THERE FOR YOUR PEOPLE

5.3 STICK TO YOUR VALUE

5.4: BE YOURSELF

CHAPTER 6. COLLABORATIVE

 LEADERSHIP

Ron desantis

6.1 BUILDING ALLIANCES WITH LEGISLATURE
TO PROTECT FLORIDANS' FINANCIAL FUTURE
AND ECONOMIC LIBERTY
          CHAPTER 7. PUBLIC RECEPTION AND
                                APPROVAL
7.1 APPROVAL RATING
7.2 POPULARITY COMPARED TO OTHERS
7.3 ACCESSING IMPACT ON FLORIDIAN
CONCLUSION

Ron desantis

INTRODUCTION

In the intricate world of American politics, few
individuals have garnered as much attention as Ron
DeSantis, the Governor of Florida. Beyond the realm of
policies and partisan debates, DeSantis's approach to
leadership stands out as a compelling force that not only
shapes the trajectory of his state but also influences the
broader national discourse. This publication delves into
the complexities of "Ron DeSantis's Leadership Style:
Strategies and Decision-Making Approaches," providing
a thought-provoking exploration into the fundamental
principles, strategic maneuvers, and philosophical
foundations that define his distinct approach to
governance.

Ron desantis

As we embark on this literary journey, we will uncover the various facets of DeSantis's leadership style, examining how he navigates the challenges of modern politics with a unique combination of assertiveness and pragmatism. From his early years and formative experiences to the pinnacle of his tenure as governor, each chapter peels back the layers of his decision-making processes, shedding light on the strategies employed to address critical issues facing Florida.

Drawing upon a diverse range of anecdotes, interviews, and policy analyses, this publication aims to provide readers with a nuanced understanding of DeSantis's leadership philosophy. Whether it is tackling public health crises, steering economic policies, or engaging in

Ron desantis

global affairs, we will explore the methodologies, values, and considerations that guide his decision-making.

Ultimately, "Ron DeSantis's Leadership Style" seeks to contribute to a deeper comprehension of the man behind the policies, offering readers an enlightening journey into the strategic mindset of a leader who continues to shape the political landscape with his unique and influential approach.

CHAPTER 1. Who is Ron Desantis?

Ron DeSantis is an American politician who has held the position of 46th governor of Florida since 2019. He is affiliated with the Republican Party and previously represented Florida's 6th congressional district in the U.S. House of Representatives. The representaton was betweeen 2013-2018. Ronald Dion DeSantis, commonly known as Ron DeSantis, also ran for the 2024 Republican presidential nomination but withdrew his candidacy in January 2024.

Born in Jacksonville, Ron DeSantis spent most of his childhood in Dunedin, Florida. He pursued his education

Ron desantis

at Yale University and Harvard Law School. In 2004, he joined the United States Navy and achieved the rank of lieutenant. During his time in the Navy, he served as a legal advisor to SEAL Team One and was stationed at Joint Task Force Guantanamo in 2006. He was later deployed to Iraq in 2007. Upon returning to the United States, Ron DeSantis served as a special assistant U.S. attorney at the U.S. Attorney's Office in the Middle District of Florida until his honorable discharge from active military duty in 2010.

In 2012, Ron DeSantis was elected to Congress and successfully secured reelection in 2014 and 2016. He played a significant role as a founding member of the Freedom Caucus and was recognized for his close association with President Donald Trump. Ron DeSantis briefly entered the race for the U.S. Senate in 2016 but withdrew when incumbent Senator Marco Rubio decided to seek reelection. In the 2018 gubernatorial election, he won the Republican nomination and narrowly defeated the Democratic Party nominee, Tallahassee mayor Andrew Gillum, by a margin of 0.4% in the general election.

Throughout the COVID-19 pandemic, as well as during the occurrences of Hurricane Ian and Hurricane Nicole, DeSantis served as the governor of Florida. He played a crucial role in advocating for the passage of the Parental Rights in Education Act. In the 2022 gubernatorial election, he achieved a remarkable victory over Charlie Crist, winning by a margin of 19.4 percentage points, which marked the largest margin of victory in Florida's history. DeSantis, the 46th Governor of Florida, officially assumed office on January 8, 2019, following

Ron desantis

in the footsteps of Rick Scott. Prior to his governorship, DeSantis served as a member of the U.S. House of Representatives, representing Florida's 6th district, from January 3, 2013, until September 10, 2018. He succeeded Cliff Stearns in this position due to redistricting and was later succeeded by Michael Waltz.

Born on September 14, 1978, in Jacksonville, Florida, DeSantis is a member of the Republican Party. He is happily married to Casey Black, and together they have three children. Currently, DeSantis resides in the Governor's Mansion. He pursued his higher education at Yale University, where he obtained a BA degree, and later attended Harvard University, where he earned a JD degree.

Ron desantis

Prior to venturing into the realm of politics, Ron DeSantis had an illustrious early career, particularly in the military and academia. After completing his undergraduate studies in history at Yale University, DeSantis joined the U.S. Navy in 2004 as an officer and Judge Advocate General (JAG) attorney. During his time in the military, he was deployed to Iraq, where he served as an advisor to a U.S. Navy SEAL commander.

DeSantis' military background not only provided him with a solid foundation in leadership but also shaped his understanding of national security matters. His tenure in the Navy emphasized the values of discipline and commitment, qualities that would later become evident in his political career.

Ron desantis

Following his military service, DeSantis pursued further education at Harvard Law School, where he obtained his J.D. degree in 2005. Subsequently, he worked as an advisor to a U.S. Navy SEAL commander, supporting SEAL missions. This experience in the military and as a JAG officer played a significant role in honing DeSantis' leadership skills and fostering his dedication to public service.

The combination of his military service and legal background laid the groundwork for Ron DeSantis' foray into politics, ultimately leading him to become a U.S. Representative and eventually the Governor of Florida. His early career not only highlighted his academic and professional accomplishments but also established the foundation for the principled and disciplined leadership that would define his political trajectory.

1.1 OVERVIEW OF RON DESANTIS'S POLITICAL JOURNEY

Ron DeSantis' political career has been characterized by a path that led him from military service to the halls of Congress and ultimately to the governorship of Florida. Here is an overview of the significant milestones in his political journey:

Military Service (2005–2010): Following the completion of his law degree, DeSantis served as a Judge Advocate General (JAG) officer in the U.S. Navy. He was deployed to Iraq, where he worked closely with U.S. Navy SEALs, gaining valuable experience in military law and operations.

Ron desantis

U.S. House of Representatives (2013–2018): In 2012, DeSantis was elected as the U.S. Representative for Florida's 6th congressional district. Over the course of three terms in Congress, he established himself as a staunch conservative, advocating for limited government, fiscal responsibility, and a strong national defense. His unwavering commitment to conservative principles and vocal support for these ideals garnered significant attention.

Gubernatorial Campaign (2018): DeSantis ran for the position of Governor of Florida in 2018. His campaign, closely aligned with then-President Donald Trump, placed a strong emphasis on conservative values and policies. He secured the Republican nomination and

Ron desantis

went on to narrowly defeat Democrat Andrew Gillum in the general election.

Governor of Florida (2019-present): DeSantis was sworn in as the 46th Governor of Florida in January 2019. Since taking office, he has prioritized a range of issues, including individual freedoms, economic growth, and environmental conservation. His leadership during the COVID-19 pandemic garnered national attention as he sought to strike a balance between public health measures and economic considerations.

Throughout his political journey, Ron DeSantis has maintained a prominent role in conservative politics, known for his principled approach and alignment with key Republican values. His leadership style and policy

Ron desantis

decisions continue to shape both Florida politics and the broader national discourse.

CHAPTER 2. LEADERSHIP FOUNDATION.

2.1 MILITARY INFLUENCE: THE SHAPING OF A LEADER

Ron DeSantis' military background has had a significant impact on his leadership style and approach to public service. As a Judge Advocate General (JAG) officer in the U.S. Navy, particularly during his deployment to Iraq, he gained valuable insights and values that have shaped his perspectives. Here are some key aspects of how the military has influenced Ron DeSantis.

Ron desantis

1. Leadership Development: Serving as a JAG officer provided DeSantis with a unique understanding of military law and operations. The structured and disciplined environment of the military has undoubtedly contributed to the development of his leadership skills and a strong sense of duty.

2. Combat Experience: DeSantis' time in Iraq, working closely with U.S. Navy SEALs, exposed him to the challenges and complexities of combat zones. This first-hand experience likely instilled in him a deep appreciation for the sacrifices made by military personnel and a pragmatic understanding of national security.

3. Sense of Service and Duty: Military service is often associated with a strong sense of service and duty to the nation. DeSantis's tenure in the Navy further reinforced these values, influencing his decision to transition from military service to a career in public service and politics.

4. National Defense Advocacy: Throughout his political career, DeSantis has been a vocal advocate for a robust national defense. His military background undoubtedly informs his positions on matters concerning the military, veterans, and the broader national security agenda.

5. Pragmatic Decision-Making: Military officers are trained to make quick, well-informed decisions in high-pressure situations. This pragmatic decision-making approach is likely evident in DeSantis' political leadership, particularly during times of crisis or when faced with complex policy choices.

In conclusion, Ron DeSantis' military service has left an indelible mark on his leadership style, emphasizing discipline, duty, and a pragmatic approach to problem-solving. These influences are reflected in his unwavering commitment to principles of service and his dedication to the well-being of the nation.

2.2 CONGREGATIONAL YEARS OF RON DESANTIS: EARLY INDICATORS OF LEADERSHIP STYLES.

Ron DeSantis served as the U.S. Representative for Florida's 6th congressional district from January 3, 2013, to January 8, 2018, during which he gained recognition for his unwavering conservatism and dedication to limited government. Here are the key highlights of his time in Congress:

1. Emphasis on Conservative Principles: DeSantis consistently championed conservative principles throughout his tenure. He aligned himself with the conservative faction of the Republican Party, advocating for limited government, fiscal responsibility, and a strong national defense.

Ron desantis

2. Focus on Military and National Security: With his background as a U.S. Navy JAG officer, DeSantis placed particular importance on military and national security matters. He consistently voiced support for a robust defense budget and policies that prioritized the safety and protection of the United States.

3. Opposition to Obamacare: DeSantis was a vocal critic of the Affordable Care Act (Obamacare) and actively worked towards its repeal and replacement. He advocated for free-market solutions in healthcare and aimed to reduce government intervention in the healthcare system.

4. Affiliation with the Tea Party Movement: DeSantis was associated with the Tea Party movement, a conservative political movement that emerged in response to concerns about government spending, taxation, and adherence to the Constitution. His alignment with Tea Party principles further solidified his reputation as a conservative leader in Congress.

5. Commitment to Transparency: Throughout his time in Congress, DeSantis stressed the significance of transparency and accountability in government. He supported measures to enhance transparency, such as requiring lawmakers to disclose their financial information.

6. Founding Member of the House Freedom Caucus: DeSantis played a pivotal role as a founding member of the House Freedom Caucus, a group of conservative Republican representatives. The caucus aimed to advocate for limited government, individual liberty, and adherence to the Constitution.

Ron DeSantis' congressional years were marked by his unwavering commitment to conservative principles, his focus on military and national security, his opposition to Obamacare, his affiliation with the Tea Party movement, his dedication to transparency, and his role in the House Freedom Caucus.

CHAPTER 3. CORE PRINCIPLES AND VALUES.

3.1 COMMITMENT TO INDIVIDUAL FREEDOMS.

Throughout his political career, Ron DeSantis has consistently demonstrated a steadfast dedication to safeguarding individual freedoms. This unwavering commitment is evident in a multitude of policy decisions and public statements.

- COVID-19 Response: DeSantis gained widespread attention for his approach to the

COVID-19 pandemic, which emphasized personal responsibility and opposed stringent lockdown measures. He prioritized the preservation of businesses and empowered individuals to make their own informed decisions regarding health precautions.

- Vaccine Distribution: DeSantis placed great importance on respecting individual choice when it came to COVID-19 vaccinations. He steered clear of imposing mandatory vaccine mandates and instead encouraged voluntary participation in vaccination efforts.

- Executive Orders: The governor issued executive orders aimed at safeguarding individual liberties.

Notably, he prohibited the implementation of COVID-19 vaccine passports and prevented local governments from imposing restrictive measures that could infringe upon personal freedoms.

- Education Choice: DeSantis staunchly supports initiatives that promote school choice, granting parents the freedom to select the educational options that best suit their children's needs. This includes the ability to choose between public, private, and charter schools.

- Second Amendment Rights: DeSantis consistently champions the rights enshrined in the Second Amendment, advocating for policies that protect law-abiding gun owners and their constitutional rights.

These examples serve as a testament to DeSantis' unwavering dedication to preserving individual freedoms, whether they pertain to public health, education, or personal rights.

Ron desantis

3.2 ECONOMIC PHILOSOPHY:GROWTH AND PROSPERITY.

Ron DeSantis's economic ideology revolves around promoting growth and prosperity by implementing pro-business strategies. His objective is to boost economic progress by minimizing regulations, reducing taxes, and establishing a favorable environment for businesses. DeSantis firmly believes that these actions will attract investments, foster job creation, and ultimately enhance the overall growth and prosperity of the state. His emphasis on limited government intervention aligns with a conservative economic approach, highlighting the significance of the private sector in driving economic triumph.

3.3 ENVIRONMENTAL STEWARDSHIP

Governor Ron DeSantis has demonstrated a strong dedication to protecting the environment in Florida. Specifically, he has implemented measures to tackle environmental issues like water quality and red tide. DeSantis has initiated programs aimed at enhancing water management and restoration endeavors, allocating resources to combat detrimental algal blooms. Furthermore, he has provided funding for projects focused on restoring the Everglades, highlighting the significance of safeguarding Florida's distinct ecosystems. DeSantis has also voiced his endorsement for renewable energy initiatives and conservation

Ron desantis

strategies, illustrating a well-rounded approach to environmental policies.

CHAPTER 4. DECISION MAKING-FRAMEWORK

4.1 PRAGMATISM IN POLICY CHOICES.

Governor Ron DeSantis has demonstrated a pragmatic approach when it comes to making policy decisions. He has consistently prioritized conservative principles and has focused on addressing issues that are in line with his political priorities. Here are some key areas where his policy choices have been evident:

Ron desantis

- Economic Policies: DeSantis has been a strong advocate for pro-business policies. He has implemented tax cuts and regulatory reforms that aim to stimulate economic growth and foster job creation.

- COVID-19 Response: Throughout the pandemic, DeSantis has taken a targeted approach. His main focus has been on protecting vulnerable populations and avoiding strict lockdown measures. He has emphasized personal responsibility, efficient vaccine distribution, and the need to maintain economic activities.

- Education: DeSantis has been a vocal supporter of school choice initiatives. He has also worked towards increasing funding for teacher salaries and implementing reforms to enhance the overall quality of education in Florida.

- Environment: DeSantis has made significant efforts to address environmental challenges in the state. He has allocated funds for Everglades restoration, taken steps to combat algae blooms, and implemented initiatives to safeguard Florida's natural resources.

- Criminal Justice: DeSantis has consistently shown support for law enforcement and has taken a tough stance on crime. He has implemented policies aimed at enhancing public safety and addressing the need for criminal justice reform.

Understanding Governor DeSantis' practical approach requires careful consideration of these specific policy choices. It is important to recognize that these choices align with conservative values and reflect his vision for effective governance in Florida.

4.2 CRISIS MANAGEMENT: DESANTIS RESPONSE TO CHALLENGES.

Governor Ron DeSantis has encountered a range of challenges throughout his tenure, including significant instances of crisis management:

- COVID-19 Pandemic: DeSantis adopted a distinctive strategy by striking a balance between public health and economic concerns. Instead of implementing strict lockdowns, he prioritized targeted measures to safeguard vulnerable populations, expedited the distribution of vaccines, and ensured the continuation of economic activities.

- Hurricane Preparedness: Given Florida's susceptibility to hurricanes, DeSantis has displayed a proactive approach to preparedness and response. He has effectively coordinated efforts between state and local agencies, promptly providing the necessary resources for evacuation and recovery.

- Environmental Issues: DeSantis has actively addressed environmental challenges, such as

toxic algae blooms and Everglades restoration.
By allocating funds and implementing policies,
he has worked towards mitigating the impact of
these issues, demonstrating his commitment to
environmental crisis management.

- Infrastructure Resilience: DeSantis has
  prioritized infrastructure improvements to bolster
  the state's resilience against natural disasters.
  This includes investments in water infrastructure
  and tackling concerns like sea-level rise.

His crisis management approach encompasses proactive
planning, strategic allocation of resources, and a
willingness to make decisions that align with his political
philosophy while considering the well-being of Florida's

residents. It is important to acknowledge that opinions on his responses may vary depending on individual perspectives and priorities.

4.3 TRANSPARENCY

Governor Ron DeSantis has faced scrutiny regarding the level of transparency during his time in office. Although his administration has made efforts to provide information to the public, critics have expressed concerns about certain aspects:

- COVID-19 Data Reporting: There have been instances where the transparency of COVID-19 data reporting has been questioned. Some critics argue that the state's reporting practices may not have accurately reflected the full impact of the pandemic.

- Public Records Requests: Critics have raised issues regarding delays or difficulties in obtaining public records through Freedom of Information Act requests. This has led to suggestions that certain government processes may lack transparency.

- Media Access: DeSantis has faced criticism for his interactions with the media, with claims that access to information or press briefings may be limited or managed in a way that some perceive as lacking transparency.

It is important to acknowledge that opinions on transparency can vary, and different stakeholders may have differing views on how open and accessible the administration has been. When evaluating transparency, it is crucial to consider multiple perspectives and the evidence available.

4.4 ACCOUNTABILITY

As the Governor of Florida, Ron DeSantis bears the responsibility for a range of duties, which include:

- Policy Decisions: DeSantis is tasked with making crucial decisions regarding state policies, encompassing areas such as healthcare, education, and the economy.

Ron desantis

- Emergency Response: The governor is accountable for effectively managing and responding to emergencies, be they natural disasters or public health crises.

- Budget and Finances: DeSantis actively participates in the state budget process, determining spending priorities and establishing fiscal policies.

- Executive Appointments: It is within the governor's purview to appoint key officials and heads of state agencies, a significant aspect of his responsibilities.

- Legislation: While the Florida Legislature is responsible for passing laws, the governor possesses the ability to influence the legislative process by proposing bills and utilizing the power of veto.

- Representation: DeSantis represents the state in various capacities, both nationally and internationally, ensuring Florida's interests are advocated for.

- Constituent Services: Addressing the needs and concerns of Florida residents is an essential aspect of the governor's role, ensuring their voices are heard and their issues are addressed.

Ron desantis

The governor's accountability for these responsibilities is reinforced by public scrutiny, media coverage, and the electoral process.

CHAPTER 5. COMMUNICATION STRATEGIES

Ron DeSantis, the current governor of Florida, has demonstrated his exceptional communication skills when it comes to leading the state. Despite facing numerous challenges in recent years, such as the pandemic and economic downturn, DeSantis has consistently conveyed a message of strength and stability to the people of Florida. He has employed various tactics to effectively communicate his vision and connect with individuals from all political backgrounds.

5.1 STAND UP FOR YOUR BELIEFS

One of his most significant actions is advocating for his beliefs, regardless of opposition from any source. A

Ron desantis

prime example of this is his clash with Disney regarding the state's "Don't Say Gay" legislation. Despite facing significant backlash, DeSantis remained steadfast and determined. He persisted in championing the bill and defied Disney's opposition by enacting it into law.

Many individuals in his position might have hesitated to challenge such a formidable corporation, but not DeSantis. He firmly believed that his actions were in the best interest of Florida, and he fearlessly defended his stance.

Other companies can learn from DeSantis' approach and demonstrate unwavering conviction, even when it contradicts popular opinion. It requires courage, but taking a resolute stand reinforces one's position as a leader. Moreover, it garners considerable attention.

5.2: BE THERE FOR YOUR PEOPLE

The way DeSantis handled the pandemic will forever be etched in the minds of Floridians. While some governors opted for shelter-in-place orders and business closures, DeSantis adopted a distinct approach.

He chose to keep Florida open, despite the subsequent increase in COVID cases, and refrained from implementing a statewide shutdown. He prioritized providing resources to businesses and individuals facing hardships and made sure that everyone had access to vaccinations.

Ron desantis

DeSantis has consistently demonstrated his commitment to the people of Florida. He regularly held press conferences to keep them informed about the ongoing situation and willingly addressed even the most challenging questions.

In today's corporate landscape, it is crucial to be present for your team. Employees seek guidance and support from their leaders, so it is essential not to disappear during challenging times. Make yourself available to answer questions and address concerns. Your employees will value this and remain dedicated to their work.

5.3 STICK TO YOUR VALUE

Ron DeSantis is known for his brevity in speech, which makes his words all the more impactful. This is because he is a man of unwavering conviction.

For instance, DeSantis is a staunch advocate for the environment, and he has consistently prioritized investing in environmental causes. This includes initiatives such as the restoration of America's Everglades, the preservation and expansion of wildlife corridors, and the protection of Florida's invaluable waterways.

Regardless of one's personal beliefs, it is crucial to remain steadfast in them. By doing so, you will earn the respect of employees, customers, and investors alike. You will be recognized as an individual who stands for something, even if it deviates from the conventional party line.

5.4: BE YOURSELF

Ron DeSantis can be best described as "genuine" if we were to summarize him in one word. He fearlessly presents his true self and is unafraid to take a stance that may not be popular. This authenticity has proven to be advantageous for him and is something that garners admiration from others. In a realm where politicians often strive to please the majority, DeSantis is seen as a breath of fresh air.

Ron desantis

Being authentic holds significant value in the business world. Both employees and customers possess the ability to discern insincerity, so it is crucial not to pretend to be someone you are not. Instead, strive to be genuine in your interactions, and you will find that people will respond positively.

Ron desantis

CHAPTER 6. COLLABORATIVE LEADERSHIP

6.1 BUILDING ALLIANCES WITH LEGISLATURE TO PROTECT FLORIDANS' FINANCIAL FUTURE AND ECONOMIC LIBERTY

Today, Governor Ron DeSantis officially signed comprehensive legislation aimed at safeguarding the people of Florida from the corporatist environmental, social, and corporate governance (ESG) movement. This movement, which has gained global traction, seeks to impose woke political ideology within the financial sector, prioritizing politics over the fiduciary responsibility to make sound financial decisions for beneficiaries. The governor's decision to enact this legislation aligns with his earlier proposal announced earlier this year.

Governor Ron DeSantis stated, "In Florida and throughout the country, we have heard from law-abiding small business owners and consumers who have faced discrimination in accessing financial services due to their occupation or personal beliefs. Through this legislation, Florida will continue to lead the nation in opposing the influence of major banks and corporate activists who have colluded to inject woke ideology into the global marketplace, disregarding the financial well-being of beneficiaries."

Ron desantis

Chief Financial Officer Jimmy Patronis added, "Just as
the Governor successfully challenged Dr. Fauci and
emerged victorious, he is now taking on a
WOKE-WALL Street that condescends to everyday
Americans. WOKE-Wall Street seeks to align itself with
the CCP and Dylan Mulvaney! Despite the disdain
shown by left-wing media towards Florida, people are
flocking from the Blue States under Governor DeSantis'
leadership! Our firm stance against ESG sends a clear
message to the world that Florida embraces prosperity,
cherishes freedom, and is a place where WOKE ideology
meets its demise."

House Speaker Paul Renner emphasized, "Florida will
not succumb to the political posturing of wealthy elites.
Corporations have no right to circumvent our democratic
process. Companies that engage in ESG practices harm

their customers and the communities they serve, including Florida's retirees, by driving up the cost of their products. I commend Governor DeSantis for standing up to corporate giants who believe they are above the law and for safeguarding the hardworking people of Florida."

The State Board of Administration, under the guidance of Governor DeSantis, has implemented measures to ensure that investment decisions are based solely on financial factors and do not prioritize ESG considerations at the expense of investment returns. These requirements have been extended to all state and local funds. Additionally, state and local governments are now prohibited from using ESG factors when issuing bonds, and rating agencies that negatively impact bond ratings due to ESG ratings are also prohibited. Furthermore, ESG considerations are not allowed in the procurement and contracting processes for all state and

Ron desantis

local entities. Banks engaging in corporate activism are now prohibited from holding public deposits as a qualified public depository. Financial institutions are also prohibited from discriminating against customers based on their religious, political, or social beliefs, including their support for border security, firearm ownership, and energy independence. The financial sector is no longer allowed to consider "Social Credit Scores" in banking and lending practices, which could hinder Floridians from obtaining loans, lines of credit, and bank accounts. To ensure compliance, the Attorney General, Chief Financial Officer, and Commissioner of Financial Regulation have been directed to enforce these provisions to the fullest extent of the law. These legislative accomplishments reflect the actions taken by Governor DeSantis and the SBA trustees to prioritize financial considerations in investment decisions. The full resolution can be found here.

CHAPTER 7. PUBLIC RECEPTION AND APPROVAL

7.1 APPROVAL RATING

In January 2024, a survey revealed that approximately 30 percent of Americans held a highly unfavorable opinion of Florida Governor Ron DeSantis, while 15 percent of Americans had a very favorable view. DeSantis actively campaigned for the 2024 Republican presidential nomination from May 2023 until his announcement in January 2024 that he would be withdrawing from the race.

1. Ron DeSantis' job approval.

Ron desantis

Regarding his job approval rating, in July, a majority of
Florida voters expressed their approval of DeSantis'
performance as governor. However, the latest FAU poll,
released on Thursday, indicated that the governor's
approval in the state was nearly evenly divided, showing
a decline of approximately four percentage points over
the course of four months. This decline was highlighted
in a larger report that projected Donald Trump's victory
over DeSantis in Florida's presidential primary, despite a
growing number of Florida voters holding unfavorable
views of the former president. The results were obtained
through a survey conducted by Mainstreet Research,
which involved 946 registered voters across all regions
of Florida from October 27 to November 11.

While these figures provide a snapshot of public opinion
at a specific moment, they indicate a downward trend in

Ron desantis

the governor's approval rating within his home state, particularly among certain demographic groups. When DeSantis won his reelection by a significant margin one year ago, he garnered support from a diverse coalition of voters, including independents, women, and Hispanics. However, the recent poll shows that nearly 60 percent of respondents disapprove of the job he is currently doing as governor, marking an increase of nearly 14 points since July.

DeSantis initiated his presidential campaign in May following the passage of several conservative priorities by the GOP-led Legislature, such as a law that made it more challenging for undocumented immigrants to work in Florida and a six-week abortion ban. Since then, DeSantis has divided his time between the campaign trail and his duties as governor, with a significant portion spent outside of the state, particularly in Iowa, where he has been actively courting voters. Over this period, his favorability ratings have declined among women by 8 percentage points and slightly among Hispanics by 4.5 points.

7.2 POPULARITY COMPARED TO OTHERS

According to the latest morning consultation survey, Ron DeSantis is ranked among the 10 least liked governors in the United States. Interestingly, the survey also indicates that Iowa's chief executive has not benefited from his proximity to the Florida governor. While DeSantis and every other governor included in the poll have a positive approval rating in their respective states, DeSantis's approval stands at 51%, with a corresponding disapproval rate of 45%. In comparison, Republican governors like Phil Scott of Vermont (83% approval, 14% disapproval) and Chris Sununu of New Hampshire

Ron desantis

(67% approval, 25% disapproval) enjoy significant popularity. However, DeSantis finds himself with the tenth lowest approval rating among all state leaders surveyed, sharing the same rating as New York Democrat Kathy Hochul. When considering net approval ratings that take into account unfavorable ratings, DeSantis fares even worse. Only six governors have a lower net approval rating than him, and among them, only two are Republicans. One of these Republicans, Mississippi Gov. Tate Reeves, is currently facing a competitive general election challenge from Democrat Brandon Presley, with an approval rating of 46% and a disapproval rating of 44%. The other Republican governor with a lower net approval rating is Gov. Kim Reynolds of Iowa. Reynolds has been courted by Team DeSantis as a potential endorser in the state's crucial caucuses in January. Unfortunately, Morning Consult labels Reynolds as "America's most unpopular governor," with a disapproval rating of 47%, which has increased from 39% in the first quarter of 2023. Her unpopularity has been partly attributed to a surge in negative sentiment among independent and Republican voters, particularly due to her signing of a strict anti-abortion law.

7.3 ACCESSING IMPACT ON FLORIDIAN RERESIDENTS

- **Putting Students, Families, and Teachers First**

Historic Investments in Florida's Education System:

We achieved and ensured the highest ever per-pupil spending totals at $7,793 per student, marking an increase of over $137 per student compared to the previous year.

Secured the highest ever K–12 public school funding, amounting to $22.5 billion in state and local funding, which includes $100 million specifically allocated for mental health initiatives.

Enhanced the voluntary prekindergarten budget, reaching a total of more than $400 million.

- **Pay raises for Florida teachers:**

Advocated for and successfully obtained $500 million to elevate the minimum teacher salary and provide salary increases for experienced teachers and other instructional staff, positioning Florida among the top five states in the nation for starting teacher pay.

Maintained $10 million in funding to support teacher bonuses and facilitate professional development in the field of computer science.

Ron desantis

- **Expansion of school choice options for students:**

Championed and enacted legislation to expand the enrollment capacity of the Family Empowerment Scholarship by nearly 30,000 students.

Secured an additional $42 million, bringing the total funding for the Gardiner Scholarship to nearly $190 million, thereby eliminating the scholarship waitlist. During the 2019–20 school year, the collaborative efforts of the Florida Department of Education, Step Up for Students, and AAA Scholarships resulted in over 180,500 scholarships being awarded to students with special needs, students from low- to middle-income families, students who have experienced bullying, and students facing reading difficulties.

- **Elimination of Common Core from Florida's classrooms and implementation of Florida's B.E.S.T. Standards (Benchmarks for Excellent Student Thinking):**

Formally adopted Florida's B.E.S.T. Standards by the State Board of Education, completely replacing the Common Core curriculum. These standards will be fully implemented by 2022.

- **Flexibility for families and educators during the COVID-19 public health emergency:**

Issued directives to all school districts across the state, mandating the provision of options for parents to choose between in-person or remote learning for their children.

Ron desantis

Extended the deadline for students to achieve the minimum qualifying SAT or ACT scores required to obtain a Bright Futures scholarship.

The Florida Civics and Debate Initiative (FCDI) was established in collaboration with the Florida Department of Education and the Marcus Foundation. Its primary goal is to enhance the civic knowledge, skills, and disposition of middle and high school students. With a generous $5 million grant from the Marcus Foundation, the initiative aims to expand debate and speech programs in all public school districts across Florida. Moreover, it provides support for exceptional teachers who play a pivotal role in shaping students into responsible citizens, thereby safeguarding our constitutional republic for future generations. To date, the FCDI has witnessed the participation of nearly 700 students from 105 schools in nine regional competitions. Additionally, 12

regional educators have been appointed as statewide ambassadors, and over 80 Florida educators have become coaches. Since its inception, the FCDI has witnessed an impressive 83% average increase in speech and debate participation in the South and Central Florida regions combined.

Florida's higher education system has consistently maintained its top position in national rankings. According to U.S. News and World Report, Florida has been ranked as the leading state in the nation for higher education for three consecutive years. Notably, three universities from Florida have secured positions in the top 50 public universities list: the University of Florida (6), Florida State University (19), and the University of South Florida (46).

Ron desantis

Furthermore, I have endorsed and signed legislation that permits college student-athletes to receive compensation for the use of their name, image, and likeness. This progressive step ensures that student-athletes can benefit from their own personal brand.

Lastly, I have successfully advocated for the resumption of college and high school sports throughout the state, along with the revival of various activities such as youth sports leagues and summer camps. These endeavors contribute to the overall well-being and development of our students, fostering a sense of community and healthy competition.

- **Protecting and Restoring Florida's Environmental Resources**

Over $625 million has been secured for the protection of water resources for the second consecutive year. The allocated funds include:

1. Over $322 million for the restoration of the Everglades.
2. $50 million for the restoration of springs.
3. $160 million for targeted improvements in water quality.
4. $40 million for alternative water supply initiatives.
5. $25 million to combat harmful algal blooms and red tide.
6. Over $28 million for local water projects.

Ron desantis

Furthermore, I directed the Department of Environmental Protection to acquire 20,000 acres of critical wetlands in the heart of the Everglades, safeguarding them from potential oil drilling activities.

Additionally, I successfully advocated for President Trump to include $250 million in his 2021 budget request, specifically for the restoration of the Everglades.

Moreover, I announced an allocation of $50 million for over 20 statewide spring restoration projects, aimed at aiding their recovery and providing enhanced protection for Florida's springs.

Ron desantis

I have also championed and signed the "Clean Waterways Act," a piece of legislation that aims to minimize the impact of known sources of nutrient pollution, realign the state's resources to enhance environmental protection, and strengthen regulatory requirements.

Furthermore, I have championed and signed legislation that increases fines for sanitary sewer overflows by 100 percent and raises fines for other environmental crimes by at least 50 percent. These measures are intended to deter individuals from engaging in harmful activities and ensure that environmental investments are prioritized.

The Florida Department of Environmental Protection (FDEP) and the Florida Department of Transportation (FDOT) have unveiled their latest plans to utilize Volkswagen Settlement dollars. These funds will be used to install electric fast-charging stations along interstates throughout Florida, with the aim of promoting electric mobility and reducing fuel emissions. Under the guidance of Governor DeSantis, the state will be adding approximately 66 fast-charging stations, equipping the state's existing publicly available inventory with 168 fast chargers.

In addition to this, the acquisition of 15 Florida Forever parcels has been approved. These parcels encompass over 42,000 acres of conservation land, which will be safeguarded to preserve Florida's natural treasures for future generations of Floridians.

Ron desantis

Efforts have also been made to expedite and secure
the necessary federal permit for the Everglades
Agricultural Area (EAA) Reservoir Project's
Stormwater Treatment Area. Spanning 6,500 acres,
this project holds immense significance in the
restoration of the Everglades. It not only provides
ecological benefits but also helps reduce harmful
discharges to the St. Lucie and Caloosahatchee
estuaries while increasing the flow of clean water
southward to the Everglades.

Furthermore, a joint funding initiative between the
State of Florida and Miami-Dade County has been
announced, with a $20 million investment dedicated
to the protection and preservation of Biscayne Bay.
This funding will be utilized for crucial infrastructure
updates and the implementation of new technology,

aiding in the prediction and prevention of sanitary sewer overflows into the bay.

Lastly, grant funding exceeding $5 million has been allocated to the South Florida Water Management District and Florida Atlantic University's Harbor Branch Oceanographic Institute. This funding will support their efforts in safeguarding and studying water quality in South Florida.

Supporting Floridians Through Mental Health and Substance Abuse Initiatives

Florida's mental health services system has received a significant boost with the announcement of $23 million in funding. This funding, derived from the federal CARES Act, will strengthen the available mental health support in Florida and ensure that the

Ron desantis

Department of Children and Families can continue
providing crucial mental health and substance abuse
treatment to those in need. Out of the total funding,
$18 million has been allocated for community-based
services. This will be achieved by expanding the
capacity of the Florida Assertive Community Teams
(FACT), Community Action Teams (CAT), and
Family Intensive Treatment Teams (FIT). These
expansions will enable an additional 300 adults and
375 youth with severe mental illness to receive crisis
intervention services.

In addition to this, the Governor and First Lady have
announced that Florida is collaborating with federal
partners to allocate a portion of a previously
announced $4.9 million federal grant for peer-to-peer
counseling services. These services will specifically

cater to Florida's first responders and will be accessible through the state's 2-1-1 support system.

Under the leadership of First Lady Casey DeSantis and her Hope for Healing campaign, several funding announcements and initiatives have been launched to support Florida families. These include allocating $2 million to 18 rural Florida school districts to enhance students' access to mental health and student support services, as well as improving access to school and community-based providers. Furthermore, $5.2 million has been allocated to support telemental health services and rebuild early education facilities in Northwest Florida following the aftermath of Hurricane Michael. Additionally, nearly $5 million has been dedicated to implementing a crisis counseling program to assist Floridians in responding to the behavioral health impacts of the COVID-19 public health emergency. To extend crisis counseling services in Bay, Calhoun, Gulf, Holmes, Jackson, and Washington counties, an allocation of nearly $700,000 has been made. Lastly, a $2 million grant has been provided for the Preschool Development Infant and Early Childhood Mental Health Grant. This grant aims to enhance the skills of the early childhood workforce and improve the classroom environment.

Governor DeSantis and First Lady DeSantis have revealed that the state of Florida has secured a $5 million grant to establish a groundbreaking initiative called Support to Communities: Fostering Opioid Recovery through Workforce Development. This program aims to address the opioid epidemic by offering a comprehensive range of services, such as recovery and support programs, vocational training, and employment assistance, to individuals who have been directly affected by this crisis. The funding will be utilized to provide wrap-around support to participants, empowering them to overcome the challenges posed by opioid addiction and rebuild their lives.

- **Practicing good governance**

61 judicial appointments were made across various courts throughout the state, with a focus on expanding the representation of historically underrepresented groups, such as women and racial minorities, on the bench. Among the newly appointed judges, approximately 40% are female and nearly 30% are minorities.

Ron desantis

Furthermore, Senate Bill 1326, known as the
Department of Children and Families Accountability
Act, was championed and signed into law. This
legislation aims to reinstate a system of accountability
within Florida's child welfare system and restore the
department's role in driving performance both
internally and among all community-based care
(CBC) lead agencies and managing entity providers.

To ensure quality assurance, the DCF Accountability
Act established an Office of Quality Assurance within
the department. This office is responsible for
developing and implementing a measurable grading
scheme to monitor the effectiveness of internal
programs and contracted vendors throughout the
state.

Ron desantis

Additionally, the legislation encourages
representatives from local churches and community
organizations to actively engage in the state's child
welfare system and provide advice to the DCF on
outreach efforts. These individuals, with their
extensive networks, grassroots perspective, and
innate compassion, possess a unique ability to
support initiatives such as foster parent recruitment.

To combat the rampant corruption and excessive
spending within the Florida Coalition Against
Domestic Violence, I spearheaded the effort to
introduce and ultimately pass legislation that would
remove them from the Florida Statutes. This crucial
legislation now grants the Department of Children
and Families the authority to oversee all programs
related to domestic violence services. By doing so, we
are restoring accountability within our government
and ensuring that our most vulnerable residents and

survivors of domestic violence receive the support they need.

In a significant development, I am pleased to announce that the Agency for Health Care Administration has officially submitted its Section 804 Importation Proposal (SIP) to the U.S. Department of Health and Human Services for Florida's Canadian Prescription Drug Importation Program. This milestone achievement is a testament to Governor DeSantis' unwavering commitment to reducing the exorbitant costs of prescription drugs for the people of Florida.

Furthermore, I had the privilege of participating in a virtual celebration commemorating the 30th anniversary of the Americans with Disabilities Act. In recognition of this momentous occasion, Governor DeSantis proclaimed July 24 as "Americans with Disabilities Act Awareness Day," reaffirming Florida's dedication to being an inclusive state for over three million individuals who face physical or mental disabilities on a daily basis. We remain steadfast in our support for these individuals and their families as they strive to achieve their aspirations.

- **Fostering Economic Development and Prosperity**
1. The Florida Department of Business and Professional Regulation has championed and approved the "Occupational Freedom and Opportunity Act," which effectively removes

obstacles for individuals seeking to enter licensed professions.

2. Through collaborative efforts, legislation was passed to establish a regulatory sandbox in Florida for fintech companies. This initiative allows disruptive companies to operate with regulatory flexibility and introduce innovative products and services.

3. A significant achievement was securing $145 million in funding for workforce development and affordable housing programs in the state of Florida's budget for the fiscal year 2020–2021.

Governor DeSantis played a crucial role in leading Florida's economic recovery after the devastating impact of the COVID-19 pandemic. In order to protect the rights of residents to earn a living and operate their businesses, he issued Executive Order

Ron desantis

20-244, which moved all 67 counties in Florida into
the final phase of economic recovery, known as
"Phase 3." This order ensured that no COVID-19
emergency ordinance could hinder individuals from
working or running their businesses, providing
much-needed certainty and stability for Floridians
and business owners alike.

Thanks to these proactive measures, Florida has
experienced consistent job growth for seven
consecutive months. Between May and November, the
state gained an impressive 721,500 private-sector
jobs. As a result, Florida's unemployment rate
dropped to 6.4% in November 2020, a significant
improvement from the 13.8% rate recorded in April.

Ron desantis

Furthermore, Governor DeSantis secured $40 million in federal funding through the U.S. Department of Labor Disaster Recovery Dislocated Worker Grant to address the challenges posed by COVID-19. This funding, administered by the Florida Department of Economic Opportunity, offers various forms of assistance to eligible Floridians, including temporary jobs, employment and training services, and supportive services. Those who qualify for this disaster-relief employment encompass dislocated workers, individuals who have been temporarily or permanently laid off due to COVID-19, self-employed individuals who have lost work because of the pandemic, and those facing long-term unemployment.

Ron desantis

Governor DeSantis' proactive approach and successful implementation of economic recovery measures have undoubtedly made a significant impact on Florida's ability to bounce back from the hardships caused by the COVID-19 public health emergency.

Legislation has been enacted to establish an Office of Broadband within the Department of Economic Opportunity, aimed at supporting the expansion of broadband services in underserved areas of Florida. In addition, collaboration with various private-sector companies has resulted in their relocation or expansion in the state. For instance, Scotlynn USA, a transportation and logistics company, has opened a new U.S. headquarters in Fort Myers. Synergy Technologies, a global IT consulting firm, plans to create 300 new jobs in downtown Jacksonville through a significant expansion. Furthermore,

Ron desantis

Lloyd's of London, an insurance market based in London, and Aberdeen Standard Investments have both expanded their presence in Miami. SIMCOM International, a pilot and maintenance training firm, has announced a $109 million investment in a new worldwide headquarters and training facility in Orlando, which will generate 50 jobs over the next two years.

Furthermore, there have been multiple announcements regarding the relocation of commercial aerospace companies to Florida. Made in Space will be moving their headquarters and satellite manufacturing operations from California to Florida, while Aerion Supersonic will construct a state-of-the-art campus in Melbourne.

Ron desantis

To further enhance the state's capabilities in the space and aerospace sectors, legislation has been signed to provide Space Florida with additional flexibility in financing commercial space projects. Additionally, Florida has participated in several significant launches from the Kennedy Space Center on the Space Coast. Notably, the launch of SpaceX's Falcon 9 rocket carried NASA astronauts Doug Hurley and Bob Behnken aboard the Crew Dragon spacecraft, marking the first crewed mission since the retirement of the Shuttle in 2011. Another notable launch was NASA's Perseverance Mars Rover, which is part of the Mars Exploration Program and will provide valuable information about the potential for life on the Red Planet.

Furthermore, efforts have been made to position Florida as a potential host for the U.S. Space Command, and legislation has been signed to reauthorize Visit Florida for three years, securing $50 million in funding for the current fiscal year. Additionally, a new Visit Florida marketing campaign has been launched to promote tourism in the state.

- **Keeping Florida moving**

The Florida Department of Transportation (FDOT) was instructed to expedite important construction projects in response to the slowdown in traffic caused by COVID-19. This initiative not only provided employment opportunities for the people of Florida but also resulted in a savings of more than 650 calendar days of construction time. Some of the

Ron desantis

notable projects included the Howard Frankland Bridge project in the Tampa Bay area, the widening of Southern Boulevard (S.R. 80) in western Palm Beach, and the construction at Sand Lake Road (S.R. 482) near the popular tourist area of International Drive and Universal Boulevard in Orlando. Additionally, phase one of the US-1 Cow Key Bridge construction in Monroe County, the Diverging Diamond Interchange on S.R. 200 (A1A) at I-95 in Nassau County, and the creation of five new I-4/S.R. 408 flyover ramps for the I-4 Ultimate Project in Orlando were also part of this endeavor.

Furthermore, significant funding of over $9 billion was secured for the State Transportation Work Program to carry out various transportation infrastructure projects across the state. This included

$2.5 billion for highway construction, encompassing the addition of 101 new lane miles. Moreover, over $120 million was allocated for seaport infrastructure improvements, $400 million for aviation enhancements (including $85 million for spaceports), and $885 million for rail and transit projects. Additionally, more than $430 million was dedicated to the repair and replacement of bridges.

To enhance safety, the FDOT introduced Operation STRIDE (Statewide Traffic and Railroad Initiative using Dynamic Envelopes) in December 2019. This initiative aimed to prevent further fatalities at or near rail crossings on state roads and state-owned land crossings.

Lastly, a statewide workforce development program was launched to establish career paths in transportation construction, thereby creating opportunities for individuals to build a successful future in this industry.

- **Maintaining Florida's Fiscal Health and Safeguarding Taxpayer Dollars**

Florida families have benefited from more than $350 million in tax relief, which includes measures such as property tax relief, a 3-day back-to-school sales tax holiday, and a 7-day disaster preparedness holiday. In response to the financial impact of the COVID-19 public health emergency, decisive fiscal action was taken. This involved vetoing $1 billion from the state's fiscal year 2020-2021 budget and implementing agency budgetary holdbacks to

Ron desantis

safeguard Florida's financial stability. Despite the financial uncertainty caused by COVID-19, Florida has managed to maintain its strong 'AAA' bond rating through prudent fiscal management.

- **Recovering from and safeguarding against disasters**

acquired $1.3 billion in federal and state funding to aid communities across the state in their endeavors to respond to, recover from, and mitigate against significant disasters and emergencies.

obtained more than $730 million in federal Community Development Block Grant Disaster Recovery funds, which will be allocated to the counties affected by recent hurricanes to support their recovery efforts.

revitalized the Hurricane Michael Recovery Homebuyer Loan Program, offering $10 million in down payment assistance to Floridians who have been impacted by Hurricane Michael.

instructed the Florida Division of Emergency Management to expedite hurricane recovery funds to assist counties and communities affected by hurricanes. Consequently, Florida has disbursed over $3.5 billion in hurricane recovery funds since January 2019, including $2.6 billion in FEMA Public Assistance funding, which expedites the rebuilding process for counties after a disaster.

established a partnership with the U.S. Department of Agriculture (USDA) to administer more than $380 million in grant funding for Florida's timber industry following the aftermath of Hurricane Michael.

obtained approval from the Federal Emergency Management Agency for individual assistance for counties impacted by Hurricane Sally.

coordinated statewide response efforts for multiple storms during the unprecedented 2020 Atlantic Hurricane Season, including Hurricanes Isaias, Laura, Sally, and Eta.

initiated a comprehensive "Know Your Zone, Know Your Home" campaign, incorporating radio and television advertisements, to educate Floridians on hurricane safety during the COVID-19 pandemic.

- **Protecting Floridians through the Rule of Law**

Introduced the "Combatting Violence, Disorder, and Looting and Law Enforcement Protection Act," a legislative proposal aimed at establishing new criminal offenses and imposing stricter penalties on individuals who target law enforcement and participate in violent or disorderly assemblies.

Allocated significant resources to bolster local law enforcement efforts, including the deployment of 700 Florida National Guard soldiers and the assignment of 1,300 sworn Florida Highway Patrol troopers. These measures were taken to safeguard Florida communities and businesses.

Advocated for and enacted legislation mandating government employers and businesses to adopt the "E-Verify" electronic verification system. This move ensures a secure and lawful labor market in Florida.

Ron desantis

Implemented the Federal 287(g) Program in collaboration with the Florida Department of Corrections and U.S. Immigration and Customs Enforcement. This initiative enhances public safety by identifying criminal illegal aliens who are received into correctional facilities.

Established the Florida Foundation for Correctional Excellence (FFCE), a direct support organization aimed at fostering partnerships between the public and private sectors. The FFCE's primary objective is to increase investment in re-entry programs and workforce training for inmates.

Secured funding of over $2 million and the creation of 10 positions to implement the Statewide Behavioral Threat Assessment Strategy within the Florida

Ron desantis

Department of Law Enforcement (FDLE). This strategy aims to enhance public safety by proactively identifying potential threats and addressing them effectively.

Ensuring Election Security and Efficiency

In 2020, we successfully collaborated with local governments and supervisors of elections to administer three statewide elections. Through the Joint Election Security Initiative (JESI), we implemented improvements based on lessons learned and enhanced communication between counties and the Department of State. To address crucial issues identified by the Supervisors of Elections for the 2020 election season, Executive Order 20-149 was issued. This order focused on maximizing voter safety, increasing poll workers, and expanding polling locations. Additionally, we allocated $10 million for state-level election oversight activities, with a specific

Ron desantis

emphasis on enhancing cybersecurity in Florida's election system. This included funding for cybersecurity positions, initiatives, list maintenance services, voter outreach, constitutional amendment advertisements, and election security grants.

Assisting Florida's Military and Veterans

Continued to offer pro bono legal services to active duty service members in Florida through the Governor's Initiative on Lawyers Assisting Warriors (GI LAW) program, which has assisted more than 120 individuals to date.

I took part in the "Governor's Challenge to Prevent Suicide Among Service Members, Veterans, and Their Families," a nationwide call to action aimed at

Ron desantis

implementing the best practices and policies for
suicide prevention.

Successfully obtained nearly $30 million in the state
budget for the benefit of Florida's military presence
and families, including:

$2 million for the Florida Defense Support Task
Force.

$6.2 million for the reconstruction of the Panama
City Armory following the destruction caused by
Hurricane Michael.

$4.2 million to support Florida National Guardsmen
and women pursuing higher education degrees.

$8.4 million to provide scholarships for children and
spouses of deceased or disabled veterans.

Enacted legislation to establish a new specialty license plate with an annual use fee that benefits the non-profit Florida Veterans Foundation.

Collaborated with the American Legion of Florida to create the COVID-19 Project Vet Relief Fund, in which the FDVA participated. This fund offers emergency assistance to veterans affected by the public health emergency.

Introduced paychecks for Patriots hiring fairs in partnership with the Florida Department of Economic Opportunity. These fairs aim to connect veterans and military family members with numerous employers across the state.

Ron desantis

Secured $2 million for Veterans Florida to fulfill the duties and responsibilities mandated by the legislature for the VETS Program. This program encompasses career, workforce, and entrepreneurship training.

Signed legislation enabling veterans and active duty service members to expedite their degree completion without redundant course requirements.

Announced an allocation of $8 million for the "Salute Our Soldiers" Military Loan Program, which provides down payment and closing cost assistance, along with low-interest rate first mortgages, to veterans and active-duty military personnel.

Successfully obtained over $20 million for the final phases of co.

Leadership During the COVID-19 Public Health Emergency

In Florida's history, Governor DeSantis has overseen the largest emergency activation response at the state level in 2020. Throughout the public health emergency, the governor prioritized the safety of our state's most vulnerable residents and led the implementation of a series of executive orders that established sensible and data-driven policies. These measures were aimed at ensuring a deliberate and targeted approach to containing the spread of COVID-19 in Florida.

Ron desantis

By mobilizing all available resources within the state government, Governor DeSantis entrusted the Florida Division of Emergency Management, the Florida Department of Health, and the Agency for Health Care Administration with a comprehensive approach to support Florida's hospital system, 67 county health departments, and 4,000 long-term care facilities. These agencies collaborated with federal, private, and non-profit partners to address the needs of Floridians.

Since the onset of the public health emergency in Florida, Governor DeSantis has taken prompt and decisive action to safeguard our state's most vulnerable populations. This includes individuals aged 65 and above, residents of long-term care

Ron desantis

facilities, and those with underlying health conditions. The governor's swift actions during this crisis have saved numerous lives and served as a model for other states and the federal government.

Ron desantis

CONCLUSION

To summarize, Ron DeSantis exhibits a proactive and assertive leadership style, utilizing strategies that prioritize effective communication, decisive decision-making, and a dedication to conservative principles. His focus on data-driven policies, as demonstrated in his handling of the COVID-19 pandemic, showcases a practical approach to leadership. Although opinions on his governance may differ, DeSantis's leadership is evidently driven by a commitment to prioritize economic factors and individual liberties, which influenced his decision-making methods throughout his time in office.

Ron desantis

www.ingramcontent.com/pod-product-compliance
Lightning Source LLC
Chambersburg PA
CBHW071053290526
45795CB00004B/1469